Portraits

Lacey Jones

NERDY KAT MEDIA

Ebook ISBN: 978-0-9861208-7-9

Print ISBN: 978-0-9861208-8-6

Copyright © 2025 by Lacey Jones

Cover: getcovers.com

Publisher: Nerdy Kat Media, LLC, P.O. Box 481, Newton, IA 50208

All rights reserved.

No portion of this book may be reproduced in any form without written permission from the publisher or author, except as permitted by copyright law.

Contents

Dedication	1
1. Elegy to Eric	3
2. Goodbye, Odie	4
3. Ghosts of Christmas Past	6
4. Compassion Fatigue	10
5. Unholy	11
6. Relinquish	12
7. Flock Plus One	13
8. Scry	15
9. Turn of An Unfriendly Card	16
10. Collosus of Dionysis	18
11. Cailleach Cove	19

12.	Ode to Tofitian Rain	21
13.	In Pacifica	22
14.	Portrait	24
15.	The Fighting Temeraire	25
16.	Tonn Chliodhna	27
17.	Capsizing the Costa Concordia	29
18.	Collapse of the Number 1 Mine	32
19.	Persephone	35
20.	Osiris	37
21.	Kicking Tires	38
22.	Swallow-Tailed Kite	39
Acknowledgments		40
About the author		41

Dedication

This book is dedicated to my sister, Rebecca (Becky), and my husband, Doug. The first ones to see my work and give honest feedback (often through their non-poker faces) and constant, unwavering support. I am blessed.

Elegy to Eric

There were bagpipes at your funeral,
befit you, Nordic god
montages of a life well lived,
it all seemed rather odd.
I wore widow's dress, front row
again, you took the stage
I don't remember much except
the sadness, smell of sage.

That person shouldn't be here
this person didn't know,
why are all these people here?
They came to see the show.
First there came the numbing
then there came the grief
final was the shattering
composure hit a reef.

Two long years of suffering
hope was crushed, grief bleeds
I'd trade my final span of life
for time to fill your needs.

Goodbye, Odie

My little old cat is dying.
His steps are awkward, eyes unfocused
and he cries when he can't see me.
I'm not sure I want to be in a world
that doesn't have my tabby Familiar.
I am feeling widowed, again.

I'm resigned to be grieving, again
outliving another love who is dying.
There's odd comfort in this ache, the strange familiar.
I gaze at him imploringly, in tears, unfocused.
He is my greatest love in our small world.
He reaches out a snow-capped paw to tap me.

Here I go again, making it all about me,
fighting to accept death must happen, again.
It seems that these past years, this is my world,
sitting by the bedside of the dying,
as they gaze at unseen figures in the room, unfocused,
but they hear them, and they smile, voices familiar.

I push my face in soft ginger fur, the scent familiar.
He always smelled like vanilla cookies, to me.
Green eyes stare into mine, they're focused.
I watch as death opaques the life from eyes, again.
I hear my husband's voice as he was dying;

"I am tired. It's time to leave this world."

Death has been a constant in my world,
an entity with which I'm too familiar.
Such a selfish act on the part of the dying,
to love me absolutely, then leave me.
I feel the empty chest constriction of grief, again.
I clutch a lifeless body, I am unfocused.

I can't see through tears, unfocused.
Odie leaves a gaping hole in my world.
I'll struggle with condolences, again.
My grief is in my chest, pain so familiar.
The last time one I loved held on to me
while completing the evolution of dying.

No longer unfocussed, I rise to greet grief, again,
it's now my world and it enfolds me,
my dark, familiar partner in the dance of dying.

Ghosts of Christmas Past

I do not fear the ghosts
of my Christmas past.
My yearly visit with each one
is a gift
a present
for this one day.

I drive out to Lantzville Beach
and bring my dog along
My mother loved dogs and beaches
I wave when I see her figure on the rocky break
sea salted, wind tangled long red hair
streaming behind her
knees tucked to her chest.
She is singing a Gordon Lightfoot song
to coax the otters into view
We sing together
that one song
and on the last note
she is gone.

I travel south to the power line
behind the rifle range
The snow shawled copse
thick with rogue fir
I see my papa, and wave to him
he stands by a lone scotch pine
I nod acceptance, and he puts his hat on top of the tree

he points out the spots to place
the seedballs I've made for the cheeky nuthatches
When the last morsel is placed,
I look at my papa, his ruddy face set in firm Scottish approval
I watch him reach for his hat from the tree
and when I look back to see his face
he is gone.

I gingerly step on the iced lake of Fourth Dam
It has seized weeping branches in a cold clutch
firmly under the water
I wave to my uncles, incautious in their immortal youth
deftly leaping over frozen tree trunks
in second-hand skates, blades sharpened by their own hands
They beckon me to join them
but my skating days are long gone
Shrugging, they race each other to the end of the lake
entering the soft, stinging mist
and they are gone.

I push my mittened hands into my pockets,
watch my dog careen from side to side
on the trail leading to Collier Dam
My dog stops beside a lone fisherman
attempting, unsuccessfully,
to put a worm on a hook.
I laugh, and my father looks up,
his thick dark eyebrow raised
in mock sternness
I sit beside him,
watching him effortlessly throw the line out

it arcs in a perfect semicircle
before breaking the glassy surface
and scattering ripples.
I look up to him, to acknowledge the beauty of the cast
but he is gone.

At Departure Bay Beach
I push the dog into the back, and move over to the passenger side
To make room for my polar bear husband.
His dark blue eyes search mine, and
when I smile,
the lines around his mouth I loved so much
deepen in happiness.

With a diamond on Christmas Eve
we pledged to be engaged forever
to live in wicked, delightful sin.
Scant years later
we broke that promise
to honour his dying wish
that he leave this world as my husband.
My eyes swim, and I push my mittens against them
when I open my eyes
he is gone.

I come home, start the playlist on my phone
and sit at the kitchen table as Liona Boyd fills the room
I do some minor patchwork with paint
on the old ceramic Christmas tree
before I begin to place multicoloured bulbs in assorted holes.
My grandmother titters in the corner

She is rocking, and reading one of those spicy Harlequin
Romances
she is obsessed with
I listen to her chide and harass the characters and
after an hour,
I put the star on top and call to her,
"Behold!"
But she is gone.

My ghosts of Christmas past will visit once a year
and in my melancholy
I am grateful.

Compassion Fatigue

Resentment looks a lot like Narcan in a sharp
and feels like it's forcing out my will.
I grab them both; Naloxone and the tarp,
the outcome undetermined by my skill.
Same guy, same place, same drug; third time today,
his unresponsive body cold to touch.
Compassion has fatigued and crawled away,
when I see something tiny in his clutch;
A crucifix, a cross is glinting gold.
Immediate withdrawal floods through his veins;
I've plunged the needle, and I tightly hold;
his bloodied eyes snap alive with pain
despite the death wish of his toxic dope,
a Savior finds him worthy of His hope.

Unholy

My cleric's collar starts to sting
a raw, red rash that won't abate
when world news of horrors bring
send thoughts and prayers and meditate

There is no accident, no chance
the predetermined outcomes state;
a child dies by circumstance
those desperate prayers won't alter Fate

The prophets false in word and deed
are fed by fear and groomed by hate
corruption absolute decreed
blind the sheep and celebrate

This collar now asphyxiates
I think it's time to separate.

Relinquish

You lock your eyes with someone in the glass,
the one who used to turn the heads of men,
accomplished flirt, a vibrant and pretty lass
with your own future quite beyond your ken.
an opaque gaze stares back without recall
no name, no memory claims your fragile mind
the mirror takes on a haunted, eerie pall,
this aging face
the years have not been kind
and hear; your heart skips strokes within your chest
but most these days you beg it; cease your beat
and let his weary body fold to rest;
so many friends and family wait to meet.
A final night has closed upon your tome,
Thanatos wakes—it's time to take you home.

Flock Plus One

Crouching among a gaggle of
dabbling Canadian geese,
a brown-skinned child pushes back
long black hair,
intent on building a tidal pool
of which he can be King.
Extending a ridiculously long neck,
a goose wades gingerly into the water,
snapping his wings forward in a fluster,
indignant with the cold.
Another approaches the boy curiously,
black eyes assessing the construction;
haughtily disinterested, it continues ambling
along the inlet.
The sporadic hiss and honking of a gander
whose life mate is being wooed by another
doesn't faze the child,
methodically tapping his palms
along the outskirts of his pond.
Another goose watches him,
unconcerned,
from her nest on a muskrat mound,
tiny hatchlings in yellow down
chirp soundlessly.
Spittles of rain dust the child's
ebony hair
and the gaggle's black feathers.

The cluster huddles around the boy,
having seemingly accepted him
as one of their own.

Scry

At night I scry with my third eye
it opens when the silence speaks
it doesn't tell me when or why
it gives me only phantom peeks.
Into the crystal orb I gaze
and Spirit gazes back at me
I follow wraiths within the haze
and whisper soft "so mote it be"
by candlelight the spell will start
by moonlight call the ghosts to talk
by daybreak I bid Spirit part
my mind has done its nightly walk.

Turn of An Unfriendly Card

Tarot 3 of Swords

I cannot empathize with a shattered heart.
That image of a fragile, breakable baby pink orb
is insulting to how I feel.
The three of swords is turned over
Unfriendly card
reveals three swords thrust into a beating heart
I feel that first blade
plunge hard, deep and cleanly.
I gasp with the pain in my chest
I feel the second as it severs sideways
and tears my heart from side to side
as grief overwhelms my shredded heart.
The third slides neatly,
down the middle until it dismembers
the connection to keeping it all together,
and I double over, sink to the floor, rock my body
and cry.
What I avoided dares me
to accept the inevitable and grow from upheaval,
become something greater than the puddle I've collapsed
into,
grow stronger from the blood-soaked earth.
The swords hurt and cause more tears as each is pulled

out
in preparation for the healing
My heart is not fragile.

Collosus of Dionysis

No tickets need be purchased to adore you
slumbering under the sultry sun,
your unfinished body of Naxian marble
dormant,
in an ancient quarry.
It is a quiet hike to worship you
Long lines of grey, green, and amber shrubs
growing a respectful distance,
throwing shade and
glowing admiration along the length of
your magnificent body.
I lay my small hand upon
your eighty-ton chest and
a flurry of euphoria infuses me,
God of ecstasy and madness,
this seaside mountain of ocean views
honors you.

Cailleach Cove

I was told, Veiled One
if I came here to die
that you would come to me
Come to me
The echo in this cave is soothing
I think I hear you
I
I have decided to die
here.
Hear
At this time
I will not let my life
of freedom and choice
be ended by a disease of disintegration
dripping into
You

My will, my mind, my body
I'm feeling tired so
I
I
will set my back against the
cool wall
Call
of this cave
I see you
You

more clearly
as my breathing slows
and my eyes close
Your white gown and hair
Share
shimmer, like this gritty
spill of
sand, that
my
My
fingers splay against.
Your pale hand is reaching for mine.
I am unable to lift it.
feel the spittle of spray
against my face and
Hand
I feel much calmer

Ode to Tofitian Rain

What is in Tofino rain
that makes it smell so sweet?
A blend of berries, a certain strain
of sea salt, fog, and peat

it smells of woodsmoke, tangy fir
and kelp washed up on shore
it smells of bitter evergreen
and dampened black bear fur,
blackberry wine that I just poured
and roasted coffee bean

it smells of maple, honeycomb
it smells of earth
it smells like home.

In Pacifica

I despise that portrait of me.
The likeness ends
with the name.
Yes, Jane Seymour, unbeheaded
Queen of England.
No, not of pinched thin lips
and sharp bird-beak nose.
Those hideous wimples
tented on over-plucked foreheads
displaying protruding toad eyes...
I was not the smoldering gypsy beauty
of Anne Boleyn
nor the loud, youthful
excess of everything
Katherine Howard
but look what their beauty cost them:
one head apiece.
I was pretty in my watchful, rich-wombed way.
I carried a King in my devoted belly
and a great love for my cousin-husband,
a fondness for estranged young Mary
and a fervent wish for peace.

I carried the scent of my beloved garden
sweet forsythia
nor the harlot's stink of
Paris and promiscuity.

I was loathe to undergo
a coronation
I did not want to be Queen
and yet here I am,
the only wife to receive a queen's funeral
and share a tomb
with the Beheader.

Portrait

This portrait of you gladdens me
It looks like you; depravity
you'd hate it, friend
it's pitiless,
displays your foul malignity.
Your smile, well
it's ominous
vampiric canine alias.
The painter tried to hide that smirk
to cover sleaze in fancy dress,
not all paint can cover murk.
He captured your peculiar quirk,
that nostril flare of snobbery
you were a nasty piece of work.

The Fighting Temeraire

I lead this Queen to a guillotine
She follows me with dignity and grace
all English oak and 98 guns.
I am an unsuitable escort for my Lady,
my low-born coarseness, the effort of towing her
punctuated
by upward belches and grinding grunts, I am unbecoming
as a royal guard
but she is silent, already haunted
She no longer flies the Union Jack as she did in battle
but a white flag of sale
and surrender
She is no longer adorned by ornament or armament
She will never again feel a storm fight to strip her sails from
her body in violent passion
her clothes have been sold
In her nakedness, she is ethereal
but I am aware of Temeraire's glorious past
The Battle of Trafalgar;
She swept to the side of the wounded HMS Victory,
and through intrepid maneuvers and savage fighting,
saved the shattered Victory from certain death,
and took two ships hostage.
But today, the sun sets in the distance on the days of
elegant,
tall-masted warships
There are streaks of red in the sky and sea, that match the

streaks of red
on her deck, that can't be washed away
I've been paid a purse of coin to escort her to the other side.
As I am reluctantly relieved of the tow ropes that bind us,
I hope that pieces of her live on somewhere
In tribute to the Fighting Temeraire.

Tonn Chliodhna

My lover haunts here, he hears me plead
with each ninth wave, I break and bleed.

I left Tir Tairngine, for Ciabhad's love,
jealous MacLir would intercede.

That deity in vengeance wrought
a spell borne from his lust and greed.

Lulled asleep, and wrapped in waves
I drowned in the harbor of Glandore sea.

I search for signs of Ciabhad,
although I've died, I am not freed.

Each ninth wave, my grieving peaks
I stack my height and gather speed.

white-capped waves of Goddess fists
hurl viciously both wood and weed.

My fingers clutch the shoreline sand,
and drag debris as I recede.

I sift through kelp, through shells and stone
and yet I know, I shan't succeed.

Banshee laments pierce the wind,
split every stone and every weed.

I am Chliodhna, I've lost my love;
with each ninth wave, I break, and bleed.

Capsizing the Costa Concordia

Divers wreathe silently through
the submerged corridors of a
140,000-ton wreck. Little fish
dark haphazardly through
the juxtaposition of tilted ballroom,
granite bars fixed in place.
Black waters lit green by headlamps
provide a surreal spotlight
for a loveseat drifting by
A vase of Chinese dollar plants poised delicately
on a marble counter.
Across the underwater tomb,
toppled chairs, tumbled together,
wait patiently to be repositioned
outside the dance floor.

There was nothing graceful about the dramatic demise
of this giantess,
listing to her death.
She was fatally wounded, being coaxed
too closely to the coast.
A hidden reef stood ground to gore
a seventy-foot gash, portside.
There was the moaning of mangled metal,
the shrieking of splitting steel,
as dark torrents were unleashed into her belly,

extinguishing her light.
"Go back to your cabins!"
and corridors flooded
"Go back to your cabins!"
and pumps failed.
"Captain! The passengers are making their own way to the lifeboats!"
echoes pointlessly through the abandoned bridge.
"Vada a bordo, cazzo!"
The Coast Guard thunders across dark waters
and the captain is stealing into his own lifeboat
to listen from the safety of shore.
Listening to the chaos,
interrupted by the agonized silence of passengers
too terrified to scream.
They hold their breath and try to calm each other
in the absence of authority.
"Vada a bordo, cazzo!"
But it's dark, he pleads, and I can't see anything...
A rope ladder is flung over the bow,
drowning passengers slinging, and
crawling crablike to Coast Guard boats
as the ship sinks to her side,
gripping thirty-seven passengers in a horrifying embrace.

Scuba-clad stewards of the dead
open the possessive clutch
of an atrium elevator
to extract bodies
protectively closed and sealed
in a grisly pantomime of protection.
The remains of the deceased

are floated to the light
to break the surface one last time.
The Costa Concordia shudders heavily,
sliding into her death repose.

Collapse of the Number 1 Mine

Deep within the underground, the caps were filled, the coal tamped down

The charge was lit, the spark died out; to drill again was the safer route

But dollars a day, dependent on load, forced safety down a different road

Time meant money, the hole re-shot; a secondary concussion caught

when the miner lit that fuse, blast on blast, all Hell broke loose.

Above the ground, the surface heaved, from every open vein smoke wreathed

mangled iron piled high, and shredded timber shot to sky

the upcast shaft purged billowing smoke, those trapped below

began to choke

Both shafts pushed the rank smoke higher, the whistle blast shrieked

the mine's on fire

Down snaking seams, the fire turned, for fourteen days the coal mine burned

Beneath the weight of water pumped, by hose and wheel, buckets dumped

metal screeched; timber rasped

the seam of Esplanade collapsed

Huddled together, a canopy of coats, they may have found solace

In prayer and in quotes,

Spades were scraped with farewell notes when afterdamp

closed miner's throats

and toxic gases rose to crests

coal dust settled over dead men's chests.

On every year, the third of May, half mast flags snap and sway

Above the plaque on Milton Street, ghosts of families silent meet

St. Peter's bells strike hard and long, pealing out a mourner's song

Shadow miners walk with kin to view the cove they're buried in

One hundred fifty lost their lives, made widows out of miner's wives

seven bodies never found

seven bodies underground

Below sea level rot particles, spikes are home to barnacles,

bullheads dark through kelp bed blooms

in the harbor

over seven men's tombs.

Persephone

Struggling
With carrying branches to dry for kindling,
Cursing
the seemingly extra long winter and those
who keep bringing it;
a shadow drifts over me like a primordial raven,
and a rush of unseen limbs streak past me.
Both alight before the barbed wire fence I keep meaning to
repair
in the spring
in the summer
in the fall.
She turns her silhouette, robed in silver fur, towards me,
I cannot see her face.
Her white hand is on Cerberus
who has one brow furrowed, watching me.
One head is cocked, listening to the sharp whistle of wind
through withered boughs
the third is panting happily,
anticipating an unrestrained romp
through chaste snow.
I bend my knee in adoration
of Persephone.
A slight incline of the hooded cloak
acknowledges my presence
and my subservience;
I am what she once was

and will never be again.
She stretches out a pallid hand,
smooth and supple for a woman of 2000 years,
this Queen of the Underworld
who executes the curses men place
upon the souls of the dead.
In the cup of her hand
glows a red pomegranate
she no longer needs.
From beneath her hood
shine orbs of quartz crystal,
I see my reflection in them
and draw closer.
Cerebus lays at the feet of his Queen,
two heads stretched out on paws,
impassively watching my progress,
the third seeking my eyes, a low growl of warning
indicating that I know my place
as subject.
I reach out upturned palms in faith
and the hood inclines again
I close my eyes,
a furious flurry of shrieking wind
envelops me.
The fury subsides. I feel the warmth of the afternoon sun.
I open my eyes to snowdrops, crowding a carpet of green
and pregnant branches thrusting their limbs
towards the sky,
and in my hand
is a pomegranate.

Osiris

"Come back from the dead," they said
"It'll be fun!" they said.
Churlish little demons are probably rolling around the floor
guffawing at the thought of me striding among my subjects,
unrecognized.
But this ghost walk amidst my children is not amusing.
Did I not teach them morality?
Yet I see, those in power to lead are frightening in their corruption.
I have more faith in the empathy
Of Yeats' rough beast than I do in the barren stare
and malignant fury
of those who have chosen to worship themselves.
And did I not teach them art and humanity?
Yet how offended they are by reason
and as equally repulsed by imagination.
I stand here, heartsick

I see no reason not to flood this earth
Again.

Kicking Tires

So that is next year's model, is it now?
The vintage being deftly moved aside.
I feel oddly sorry for them both, and how
Her sleekness won't survive the filthy ride.

The vintage is deftly moved aside,
the owner seeks his youth in pristine sheen
Her sleekness won't survive the filthy ride.
I was once the starlet in this scene.

The owner, seeking youth in pristine sheen
his hand on one, his eyes upon the next;
the vintage and the fresh, both rides I've been.
I feel oddly sorry for them, vexed.

His hand drops down, his eyes are on the next;
the Classic with her charm and Botox tried.
I feel oddly sorry for her, vexed.
Her perch, always precarious, slides.

The Classic with her charm and Botox tried
She meets my eyes, and casts her gaze askance
unsupported on that perch, she starts to slide
the modern model starts a slow advance.

She meets my eyes, and casts her gaze askance
I feel oddly sorry for them both, and how
the modern model starts the slow advance...
So, this is next year's model, is it now?

Swallow-Tailed Kite

I keep a respectful distance, entranced
by the sky painting of a swallow-tailed kite, brushing
against a grey canvas. The stark white of her belly and
sharp black
of her divided tail outline a hovering Phoenix,
she extends her thick, knuckled yellow talons and floats
to her home, fiercely gripping the nest
encircled by Spanish moss. And she turns her
forward-facing red eyes to me
locking on
and tilting her head in what I choose to feel is focused
curiosity
about this quiet, clumsy creature
who is spiritually extending a hand
in interspecies friendship.

Acknowledgments

I would like to acknowledge the tireless support and work of my editor Marci. You see something in my work that I often fail to, and you don't let me toss it aside. You bring it back up, dump it in my lap, and say in your sweetest way "go at it again. And again. And again." and this book is the result.

I also want to thank my publisher NerdyKat for taking on this book with such belief and passion. I believe in myself because you believed in me.

About the Author

Born, raised, and happily retired on Vancouver Island, Lacey finds inspiration and peace in the rugged coast, dense forests, and lush valleys of her home. She is guided by her belief in the powers of the elements around us (as above, so below). When she isn't pushing her cat Benny in a stroller along the waterfront, she is getting happily lost while wandering hiking trails with her dog Morgan.

Lacey is married to a wonderful man who tolerates (and often indulges) her bit of an obsession with the wives of Henry VIII. An English literature major, she is most content driving a forklift and slinging soil in the garden center. She is a poet, a bohemian, and a Crone whose desire to preserve Nature's surroundings inspires her writing.